HOW TO BE
FORMULA ONE
CHAMPION

HOW TO BE
FORMULA ONE
CHAMPION

RICHARD PORTER

1 3 5 7 9 10 8 6 4 2

Virgin Books, an imprint of Ebury Publishing
20 Vauxhall Bridge Road
London SW1V 2SA

Virgin Books is part of the Penguin Random House group of companies
whose addresses can be found at global.penguinrandomhouse.com

Penguin
Random House
UK

Copyright Sniff Petrol Limited 2019

Richard Porter has asserted his right to be identified as the author of this
Work in accordance with the Copyright, Designs and Patents Act 1988

First published by Virgin Books in 2019

www.penguin.co.uk

A CIP catalogue record for this book is available from the British Library

ISBN 9780753553282

This book is unofficial and is not associated in any way
with the Formula One companies.

Printed and bound in Great Britain by Clays Ltd, Elcograf S.p.A.

For D & M

CONTENTS

INTRODUCTION

If you think being a Formula One driver is just about mashing the accelerator until you are travelling very quickly, you are sadly mistaken. There are also other skills involved such as steering and braking, which, if anything, are even more important, especially if you don't want to have an accident.

But being an F1 driver is even harder than that because you can't just be good at driving round and round in circles for an hour and a half every other Sunday (March to November-ish). There are so many other abilities you have to master such as how to thank the team, how to behave at a corporate meet 'n' greet, and when to wear a branded baseball cap (clue: always).

These are just some of the basics you will need to master if you want to take part in the very top level of motorsport.

As for becoming an actual F1 champion, well that's even harder.

Formula One has been going for 69 years and in that time just 33 people have become champions. One man did it seven times and only two men have come close with five titles, all of which sounds a bit selfish, though one chap did win it once and then promptly retired before the team could ask him to have another try.

If you think becoming Formula One world champion sounds like a mighty battle of skill, strategy, teamwork, dedication, inspiration, fitness, luck and starting all interview answers with the words 'for sure' then you would be right. If you also think that it's impossible to sum up all the sweat and sacrifice required to get to the very top of an elite sport in one medium-sized book, well you would be right about that too.

But that hasn't stopped us from trying.

So pull tight those harnesses and blip that throttle because you're about to learn how to become an F1 champion ... and if you've taken the start of this sentence literally that means you're going to attempt to drive while reading a book. You're either a multi-tasking genius, in which case motorsport glory is assured, or you're a blithering idiot and your dad's Astra is about to get written off.

Either way, read on for your path to a world in which everything starts with super, from the yachts to the models to the markets you will end up opening in your twilight years. Good luck!

EARLY YEARS

GETTING STARTED

So you've decided to become a racing driver, work your way up through the formulas, become an F1 driver and then score a championship.

Well, that's great.

First of all, are you already racing in some form or other? If the answer is 'no' then ask yourself this: are you about three or four years old? If the answer is 'no' again then unfortunately it might be too late.

The top-level F1 drivers often had their first taste of karting when they were barely out of nappies and that's the sort of deep commitment you're going to need to give yourself the best shot at that Formula One championship.

The advantages to starting this young are clear: first of all, it gets all the basics of car control into your brain at a formative age; and secondly, it gives you the maximum amount of practice and experience before you make the leap into the big league. Also, at that age it's still perfectly acceptable to go 'WHEEEEEEE' when you drive fast.

But hang on, you say, how am I going to be ready to start competing in bambino karts at the age of six and move on up from there? Who can make all that possible? Well, there's a simple answer to that ...

MUM AND DAD

You're young, you're excitable, you can sit through most of a Grand Prix without going 'Ughh, Dad, this is booooooring.' You're ready to make that first move into motorsport. Before you do, however, one question: are your parents rich?

Sorry, let's rephrase that in a more sophisticated way: do your mummy and daddy have access to absolutely sackfuls of cash? Loads of it. A small fortune. If not then, sorry, this has all got a lot harder. Yes, you might be able to rise to the top in F1 if your parents aren't loaded but, let's be honest, it's a lot less likely.

Motor racing is expensive, more so than almost any other sport. If you're still in primary school and you want to get into athletics, no problem at all. Running about costs nothing. If you fancy yourself as one day becoming a top footballer then someone can probably get you an affordable ball. But unless your dear ma and pa are absolutely minted they're unlikely to respond well when you tell them that this year you want Father Christmas to bring you a £3,000 Bambino Kart and some Nomex overalls in size 6–7 yrs.

Don't be disheartened though. There are examples of kids who've come from humble backgrounds and enjoyed a rise through motorsport that only required their parents to get two extra jobs and sell the family home.

Also, who knows, perhaps you just weren't paying attention and didn't realise Daddy is one of Europe's richest petrochemical billionaires. Maybe you just didn't know that having several staff in your home is a bit unusual. Perhaps you thought all kids went to school in a helicopter. In which case, good news! You're all set on the first step to becoming an F1 champion which is, just to repeat, having parents with loads of money.

KARTING

The best way to get into motorsport is karting, and not just the sort that lets you drive a puttering skateboard in a rubber ring around a track inside a chilly warehouse on the outskirts of town in the company of 19 lads on a stag do. No, to have a serious shot at becoming F1 champion you have to start competitive karting as soon as possible in a series recognised by the CIK (Commission Internationale de Karting), which is part of the FIA (Fédération Internationale de l'Automobile) and can therefore provide two things you will need to get familiar with:

1. **An extremely dense and complicated set of rules which you soon realise you don't have the attention span to read.**

2. **A central governing body that you can moan about when things don't go your way.**

The good news is that karting provides a clear path of various formulas and these accurately mirror the structure of bigger race series in that they're quite confusing since they often change names and no one outside of motorsport is paying attention because they're all watching the F1.

In the UK, the normal progression would be from Bambino class karts (which takes you from 6 to 8 years old), to Cadet class (8 to 13), to Junior karts (11 to sitting nervously in the reception area of a major race team wearing a suit that looks far too big on you hoping it's true when they said on the phone they'd 'heard good things' about you).

Karting teaches kids many important things such as basic mechanics, elementary race craft, and how to develop a burning hatred of someone who keeps getting ahead of you in the championship while still pretending to be their friend.

Karting is also a fun way for a child to spend more time with their dad, who will be driving them all over the country in a van, furiously spannering away at a malfunctioning kart in the drizzle while a demanding 11-year-old insists it 'has' to go faster and silently hoping that the enormous sums they're spending on this endeavour pay off when the precocious little shite is able to fly them to F1 races on a private jet.

As a parent, it's important to remember this last bit and keep it in mind for all those times when your ungrateful child is claiming they 'don't want' to spend the weekend driving round in circles on an industrial estate near Worksop and would rather just hang out in the park with their friends.

DO Swerve about a bit on the formation lap because it warms up your tyres (and also because it looks quite cool on telly).

DON'T Decide to give it a bit of welly to light up the back tyres and somehow manage to stuff it into a gravel trap as this will make certain people (e.g. everyone on your team) think you can't control the car at low speed and probably shouldn't be trusted with it at higher speeds either.

BOOKS TO READ TO YOUR CHILDREN

If you're a parent hoping to guide your child on the path to becoming an F1 champion you'll have realised the importance of starting them early, and that means getting them used to the nuances and technicalities of top-level motorsport even before they're big enough to get into a kart.

To that end, here are some children's books you might want to read to them at bedtime:

- BoBo the Racing Car Finds a Slightly Faster Time in Damp Conditions

- Ronnie the Racing Driver in Thanks to My Sponsors and Their Affiliates

- A Toddler's Guide to Wet-Weather Set-Up

- Rummy Rabbit Hits a Later Braking Point at Snetterton

- Terry the Turtle's Left-Foot Braking Adventures

- A Is for Aero, B Is for Brake Balance, C Is for Clutch Bite-Point Check

- Little Gus Chicken and the Maintenance of Grip Balance on the Approach to a Hairpin

- Flubbsy & Bob Adjust the Aero Balance to Reduce Understeer at a Medium-Speed Track in Changeable Conditions

BEING FEMALE

Relatively few women end up in motorsport and one reason might be that, at the formative age when a lucky son might first get into karting, outdated gender norms in our society tend to dictate that the daughter of generous parents will instead find herself with her first pony.

That's not the only reason, of course, although it's hard to think of others unless it's something crazy like motorsport being a ridiculously outdated and sexist boys' club with a mentality locked in the 1970s. But that can't be it.

BEING BRITISH

Statistically, more F1 drivers have been British than any other nationality. The UK has, to date, fed 163 drivers into the sport, obviously not at the same time. That would be silly, much though the British like a queue.

Better yet, statistically speaking if you want to be F1 champion you're better off being from Great Britain, which has been the home nation of ten world champions – more than the next most successful nations, Germany, Brazil and Finland which have thus far managed to stump up just three champs apiece combined.

Therefore, if you want to be F1 champion it's a good idea to be from Britain, or at least pretend that you are.

THE LOWER FORMULAS

You've honed your skills in karting and you've attracted some interest from actual race-team owners and managers. Plus your voice has broken, or at least seems like it might by the time you've settled into that job at Williams.

For most drivers F1 is still a distant target but now is the time to make your move into the big-boy world of lower formulas and the lesser-spotted race series where a young talent can make embarrassing errors of judgement away from the glare of everyone except talent scouts for Formula One teams, so that's ... oh.

Bugger.

Your first foray into a motor-racing series that's a bit more grown-up than karting could be in some kind of one-make series where raw young talent gets to crash into fat old rich people who don't seem to have worked out what an apex is, or it could be in a junior single-seater series where you will be surrounded by ambitious newcomers just like you, all of whom you will grow to hate as you become consumed with a desire to destroy them.

The place you end up for your next move will depend on a variety of factors such as money, money and money. At this point it's most likely that your dad's cash, which carried you through karting, won't be enough to keep you in the lower formulas. No, most likely you're going to need some sponsorship, and that's where the hustle comes in.

THE HUSTLE

Almost every racing driver has had to develop the hustle and the longer you spend in the lower formulas the more you're going to need it to keep the cash coming in.

The truth is, racing is expensive. In fact, it's a ravenous monster that just keeps eating cash in return for tyres and testing and everything that comes with the constant desire to be at the front. The money goes out fast and comes in slow, and no one gets rich in the lower formulas. Try to overlook the team-owner parking area of the paddock, which is always conspicuously full of Porsches.

As a young driver there are no expensive road cars for you, there is only the need to keep the money rolling in so that you can immediately give it to someone else. And to accomplish that, you need to tune up your hustling skills.

The hustle is what racing drivers need to keep themselves in the game and if you don't have the hustle all the driving talent in the world won't keep you afloat.

If you've got the hustle, you'll be constantly on high alert for a new opportunity. Could be a new personal sponsor, could be a new wealthy benefactor, could be an interesting sideline in consultancy or race schooling or modelling or dog walking or whatever it takes to maintain the flow of sweet, sweet dollar.

That's why young racing drivers always need to be working the angles, charming the sugar daddies, or hunting down the factory-backed race seats in different series, just to stay racing. Because without racing, you might have to get one of those jobs that normal people have.

Unless of course you can get adopted ...

GETTING ADOPTED BY A TEAM

Some lucky drivers avoid the need for permanent hustle and get on a fast track to a potential F1 seat and, beyond that, trophies, championships and glory.

All you have to do is get spotted by the talent scout for one of the well-known Formula One teams and win a spot on their young driver programme. And to do that, all you need to do is be really, really good at driving and charming people and being nice to the team boss who will take you under his wing in a manner that might seem warmly avuncular or just child-catcher sinister (there's a fine line between the two).

If you can get adopted by a team in your younger days you'll be nurtured, trained and, of course, paid for. And then one day, all being well, you'll get that first taste of F1, which could lead to a full-time drive.

As long as you don't stuff it into a barrier on lap 1. Then they might ask for their money back.

BEING A PAY DRIVER

There's another way to dodge the hassle and potential humiliation of having to hustle your way through motorsport and that's by scoring one massive hustle result and becoming a pay driver.

A pay driver comes with a large fortune, perhaps donated by a vast corporation in their home nation because the boss wants to see one of their own people progressing into Formula One and has decided that it's you (because, after all, you're their son). With enormous corporate cash behind you, you can simply buy your way into a seat, all the way up to that Formula One drive of your dreams.

That's the good news.

The bad news is that pay drivers don't have a great history of being F1 champions, almost as if having sizeable wads of cash isn't directly related to ability. The funny thing is that, given the choice, Formula One teams would prefer to pick drivers who are good rather than drivers who come with a sack of cash from Paraguay's largest food-processing conglomerate.

Yes, the money will get you into F1 but unless you've got the racing chops to back it up there's a very real danger you'll become one of those comical seat-fillers who's forever crashing into the current world champion as he laps you or gets run over by the marshalling car or finds that his nickname is his real name with the word 'accident' crudely inserted into it.

To sum up, being a pay driver is a brilliant way to fast-track your way through the formulas to land that prized F1 seat, but it probably means you're not very good.

On balance, it might be better to hustle your way, then at least if you're crap, people won't be afraid to tell you to sod off.

DO say, 'We're so happy to have these great guys on board as sponsor. I drink it all the time.'

DON'T say, 'Blurrrrgh, get that stuff away from me, it tastes like fizzy disinfectant.'

DO thank the team for their efforts.

DON'T compare the performance of the car that they have dedicated their lives to working on to a snail/ Austin Maxi/GP2 car.

YOUR MANAGER

To help with your hustling and to boost your chances of getting adopted by a team, anyone serious about becoming an F1 champion really should have a manager by now.

Driver managers come in various types, all with pros and cons.

● AN EX-DRIVER

PROS: Used to be a professional racing driver so understands what's involved in competing at the very highest level.

CONS: Used to be a professional racing driver so has the attention span of a very fickle gnat.

• A MEMBER OF YOUR FAMILY

PROS: Knows you better
than anyone else,
blood is thicker
than water.

CONS: Might fall out with you over other matters,
e.g. your mother says you don't call enough,
your sister agrees with her that you should
take the teabags sponsorship even if it's not
'in line with your brand'.

• A PROFESSIONAL MANAGER OF RACING DRIVERS

PROS: This is what they do.

CONS: Sense they might
be diddling you.
Also, a bit
sex-pesty.

EARLY PHOTOS

As you make your way through lower race series towards Formula One it's often helpful to people (such as random strangers on the internet) if you make sure that photos of yourself at this time will seem amusing in retrospect, once you are – fingers crossed – an F1 champion.

Ways in which you might like to indulge this include:

A. Being quite spotty

B. Having bad hair

C. Sporting dubious facial hair

D. Being pudgy

E. Wearing inadvisable trousers

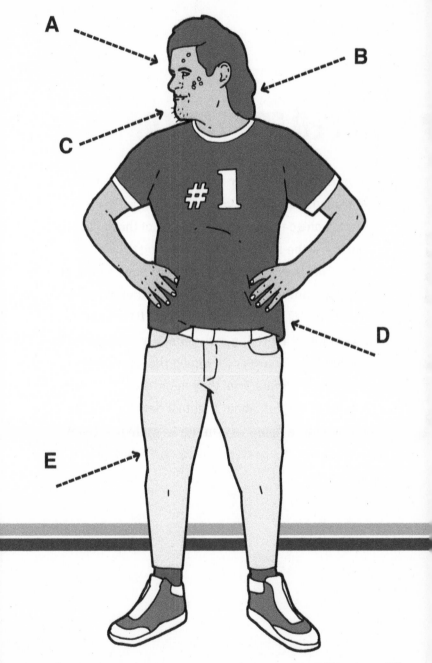

TIPPED FOR THE TOP

Some drivers in lower formulas get a certain buzz around them and, if you're going to be F1 champion one day, you need to be one of these people.

You know the sort. He's on the young driver programme, they whisper. He's got to have a shot at replacing [name of underperforming older driver currently in F1]. Back in karts, he regularly beat [name of latest F1 rising star generally considered to be brilliant]. He's currently wiping the floor with everyone in Formula Two, they might say.

A word of caution about that last one. It might be true that you're doing well in the formula just below F1 – whatever it's been renamed now – but before you get giddy on this positive buzz, have a look around you. Are you repeatedly winning at the moment not because you are brilliant but because everyone else is a bit crap? It's an easy mistake to make, and before you know it you've been bumped up to F1 where rather than covering yourself in glory you spend a season and a half clattering about at the back and whingeing on the radio before being unceremoniously binned.

So, to sum up, it's good to get a bit of a buzz about yourself humming in the background of motorsport but be careful not to believe that buzz entirely in case it turns out to be bollocks.

THAT FIRST TASTE OF F1

So you've done well in the lower formulas. People are tipping you for great things. Now you need to get yourself into an actual F1 car.

If you're on a young driver programme, that could be just a matter of hanging around the pits at F1 races with a hopeful expression and an eager-to-please demeanour, like a Labrador in a branded cap.

If you're not directly affiliated to a team it might be a bit harder but, as long as your manager is constantly 'in talks' with several team bosses (i.e. he's forever going to races and hanging around team hospitality drinking mineral water hoping to grab a five-minute chat with the boss), one day your chance may come.

This might be a try-out in an old car or, thrillingly,

this could be a go in this season's actual racing machine in a free-practice session ahead of a race. Either way, this is it, this is your first drive in a real Formula One car.

Of course, by now you've raced in a whole range of things and enjoyed ever-rising power outputs so you're going to be confident, verging on cocksure, about what you see as your destiny. Use this youthful swagger wisely. That is, channel it into a brave and brilliant few laps in which your times shame at least one of the actual drivers that season.

But don't get carried away and slither into a gravel trap on your third time round. People are watching. Powerful, influential people.

And your mum.

TEST DRIVER

Your first go in a Formula One car was probably a one-off, 'have a go and if you don't bin it we'll take it from there' trial run.

To get more experience at the very top level you need to become a test driver. Obviously, as a racer you'd rather be doing racing than spending endless hours calibrating things in the simulator and very occasionally being allowed to do some installation laps at testing or in the first free practice. But being a test driver gets you a valuable 'in' with a team and allows you to hone your skills at giving feedback to engineers in order to make the car better.

The team loves drivers who give great notes on what the car feels like and how it could be improved rather than, say, someone who leaps out and says, 'It's a bit skiddy, could you make it faster?' and then wanders off to flirt with the marketing woman from the title sponsor.

BIG BREAK

You're in with a team. You've shown that you can drive. You've shown that you can do set-up. The press say you're a promising talent. All you need is for it to happen.

Maybe the main guy gets a better offer from another team. Maybe he just gets greedy, asks for too much money next year, and accidentally 'retires' himself from a team that is trying to control its spending habit.

The rumours swirl, the meetings happen, the gossip chatters online and then, one sunny afternoon in your tiny Monaco apartment as you idly thumb through a helicopter magazine, the call comes in ...

F1
DRIVER

FORMULA ONE

Yes! You've done it! You've made it into the top drawer of motorsport.

It's time to celebrate, probably by having a protein smoothie then getting straight back to the gym and posting a photo on social media of yourself working out. There's no time for messing around because you'll need your strength for what's to come.

If you want to be F1 champion, this is where the hard work starts.

Also, for over 20 weekends a year you're going to be busy, so you might need to rearrange some plans.

● RACE NUMBER

A few years ago Formula One authorities decided that each driver had to pick a number and then stick with it. This was done for some very important reasons, such as allowing merchandise to be re-used from season to season so no one had to throw away crates of baseball caps.

When you rise to F1 you will have to choose a number and, as a racing driver, your instinct is to pick number 1. Unfortunately, that's reserved for the reigning champion so you'll have to think a bit harder. You could go for a number of personal significance, such as your birthday, your dog's age, or the number of swimwear models you've kissed. Or you could try for a number that can be worked into your name. If, for example, you're called Gianni Sevaltori you could ask for 15 and then write your name as GIANN15EVALTORI on official products. Just as long as you don't make so many driving mistakes that people start calling you "the PEN15".

● HELMET DESIGN

Now you've made it into the big league you should settle on a crash helmet design.

F1 drivers used to change their helmet livery every race until 2015 when the FIA realised that this made it hard for fans to identify their favourite drivers and was also a bit annoying. It also gave away that the average racing driver has an attention span that makes a fish seem intense.

Since you must now pick a design and stick with it, save for one 'joker' helmet per season, it's important to get it right. Ideally, your crash helmet paint scheme should include the following:

- The flag of the country you're from
- Some kind of animal to which you've been compared
- Your own signature
- Some abstract nonsense
- An overall design that is literally impossible to sketch on paper with felt tips and is completely unmemorable as a result

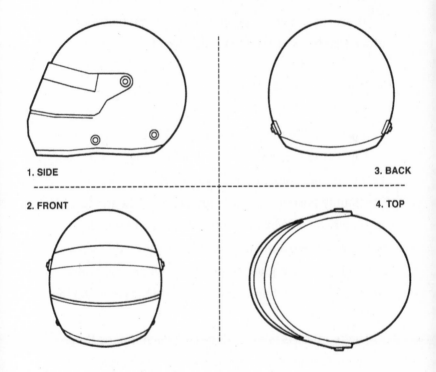

1. SIDE

3. BACK

2. FRONT

4. TOP

If you present your design and you hear anyone saying something like, 'Oh, that's attractive' or 'Wow, so simple and yet so effective', go back and start again.

YOUR TEAM

Now you're well and truly in with the big boys, and here are the important people on your team that you should probably stay on the right side of.

● *TEAM BOSS*

The guv'nor, the man in charge, the big chief.

This is the person who has ultimate power over your career at this point and who will develop a sort of pleasantly parental attitude towards you, beaming with pride when you win, defending you unconditionally when you make a mistake, adopting a tone that says, 'I'm not cross, I'm just disappointed' when you ignore team orders and then crash into your team mate on lap 37.

The team boss is often English, which means they sound milky and unconvincing when they come on the team radio at the end of a race to say well done for winning, or they are Italian, in which case they seem avuncular in a mafioso sort of way but then celebrate victories by hugging you with one hand on the back of your head, in a manner that feels incredibly threatening.

● CHIEF DESIGNER

The person credited with the overall engineering of your racing car.

You will enjoy an uneasy relationship with the chief designer because you will grow to resent the way they get credit when the car is winning but you get blamed when the car is slow, and they will view you with disdain because they regard you as the most squishy and inconsistent component in the car and the only one they can't reprogram or redesign.

Nonetheless, try not to annoy the chief designer too much or they will snap out of one of their socially awkward silences to whisper in the team boss's ear that perhaps the car would work better if you weren't in it.

● YOUR RACE ENGINEER

There are lots of engineers in the team, but this one will be your greatest ally and the person you'll spend the most time with, discussing set-up and strategy and what the people on the other side of the garage are up to.

Your race engineer will be many things – coach, confidant, comforter, punch bag – but more literally he will be an English bloke referred to by everyone using an abbreviation of their actual surname.

In all likelihood you will become closer to your race engineer than anyone else in the team, although you will never go to their house and it will be your PA who picks the extremely expensive watch you buy them for their birthday.

● PR MINDER

This is the person who will look after you whenever you are in a situation where you might be allowed to say something that could be written down or recorded.

Typically, your PR minder will be a young woman in a branded team shirt who hovers around your left elbow hoping that you don't say anything stupid.

You will either want to have sex with them, in which case you will spend all season being distractedly flirtatious in the manner of someone who is also thinking about strategy and themselves, or you will have no interest in having sex with them, in which case you will get about seven races into the season before you realise you have been getting their name wrong.

● ALL THOSE PEOPLE WHO WORK AT BASE AND DON'T GET TO GO TO RACES

You don't really know who these people are, but you should nonetheless remember to thank them every so often using the catch-all 'the guys back at the factory'.

Better yet, give them the ultimate thank you by winning a world championship, at which point in most F1 teams every employee gets a handsome bonus.

Nothing says 'Thanks, guys!' like cold, hard cash.

YOUR TEAM MATE

Of course, along with all the other people who work in your team, there is one colleague who will attract more attention than all of them put together, and possibly more attention than you (annoyingly). That is, of course, your team mate.

In Formula One this will be one of the following:

● *THE OLD FRIEND*

This is someone you've known since karting days.

You were children together, you grew up together, you were fierce but friendly rivals. Yes, you might have tussled on track in those noisy little karts but when all was said and done you could still run around together afterwards, riding bikes, eating ice cream and being best of mates in the way only the young and innocent can enjoy without complication.

You're still friends to this day, but now friends in the sense that you never see each other socially and you completely hate each other's guts.

The old friend is great inspiration for getting that F1 championship because you know how much it would irritate them if you did and at least 60 per cent of your life is now dedicated to annoying them.

• *THE ESTABLISHED FIGURE*

Someone you saw racing when you were still in karts or a lower formula, the established figure was a bit of a hero to you. That is until you had to work with them and realised what a patronising/rude/passive-aggressive twat they were and are.

Officially you say you have 'learned a lot' from them, but that isn't strictly true. They won't tell you anything or do much beyond trying to undermine you because they either think you are crap and covertly attempt to tell you this at all times, or they think you are brilliant, in which case they still try to imply you are crap because they're frightened of being overshadowed by you (see below).

The established figure does not want you to be world champion because a) that would make them look bad and b) they want to win it, possibly for another time (which just seems greedy).

• *THE YOUNG BUCK*

New to the sport, the young buck is getting all the media attention.

That's immediately annoying because the coverage is positive – unlike yours which is starting to question whether you've got what it takes to make it all the way, especially in the face of this younger challenger.

You must immediately start telling the press that this newbie brings 'fresh energy' to the team, while behind the scenes doing everything you can to undermine them.

What's particularly annoying is that technically they are the number two driver but they keep doing distinctly un-number two driver things like being faster than you and this must be stopped as soon as possible.

In many ways, the young buck is one of the biggest threats to your hope of becoming champion simply because they want to be champion too and rather rudely aren't prepared to let you have first dibs.

● *THE DUTIFUL NUMBER TWO*

Now this is more like it. The dutiful number two knows their place in the team, and that place is behind you.

When told that you are faster and they should get out of the way, they understand that message. When required, by the unspoken demands of the team, to become an unhelpful roadblock in the way of your main title rival who wants to pass so they can start crawling all over your gearbox, they are suddenly driving the widest car on the track.

And they will do all this without complaining that they don't get first go at technical improvements or that they should have some quid pro quo help in achieving victory.

Yes, the dutiful number two is your faithful, slightly downtrodden ally in your quest for a world title, all wrapped up in a personality like low-calorie margarine.

Sadly, the dutiful number two is a rare find in Formula One as most racing drivers want to win for themselves. How selfish.

• *THE EQUAL*

Perhaps the most dangerous of all the team mates, the equal is like you in every way. About the same age, about the same experience, arrived at the team at the same time.

There are no favours either way here, it's just you and him in a race to glory, like one of those horrible experiments where they seal two hungry rats in a bag. There will be no team orders, no being helpful, no extra technical assistance: this is just raw intra-team rivalry at its most powerful.

At the end of the year which of you will be world champion? The answer is neither of you, because you've spent half the season idiotically crashing into each other.

REASONS TO DISLIKE YOUR TEAM MATE SLIGHTLY MORE

- More wins
- More Instagram followers
- Better-looking girlfriend
- More lucrative endorsement deal for nicer watches/clothes/energy drink
- Simmering conviction that they're getting the better car

NICKNAMES

Many F1 drivers end up with a nickname and this can be something that really helps define you and your 'brand'.

Unfortunately, nicknames are generally not something you choose yourself and attempting to do so will make you like that kid in your year at school who suddenly announced that he wanted to be called 'Danger' and spent the rest of his school career being universally referred to as 'Dicksqueeze'. Hence, do not attempt to tell people what to call you, it will only backfire.

Obviously this is out of your hands, but here are some nicknames that sound okay and should be encouraged should they be applied to you:

LONE WOLF
LIGHTNING
POWER
HOT KNIFE
THE SLICE

Here are some nicknames that are not so good and should be ignored/not written on your crash helmet for the new season:

THE SLOTH
ROADBLOCK
CRASHMAN
THE INCIDENT
YOUR ACTUAL NAME BUT WITH 'THAT IDIOT' IN FRONT OF IT

MERCHANDISE

Merchandise is a brilliant way for your fans to show their support for you by paying an inflated sum for an item of clothing or a poster that somehow ends up mostly making your manager richer – with a small cut for you, which ends up in the murky world of your business finances.

Merchandise works best if you have one or more of the following:

- A strong racing number (see previous note on numbers)

- A distinctive feature such as striking eyes or (less likely) really thick-framed glasses

- A good nickname (see previous note on nicknames)

- A strong colour combination on your crash helmet

- A phone number for someone who owns a machine that prints T-shirts

Merchandising can be a tremendous way to satisfy your fans and keep a high profile, but do be careful about what you put your name to. For example, these are some accepted items that can be used for branded merchandise:

- T-shirts
- Mugs
- Phone covers
- Caps
- Posters
- Stickers
- Overwrought paintings of your car driving in very wet conditions looking heroic

Conversely, here are some things you should probably not sign off on when someone brings you a prototype example with your face on it:

- **Ironing boards**
- **Plasters**
- **Cushions**
- **Sea-sickness medication**
- **Anything with packaging that features the word 'urgency'**

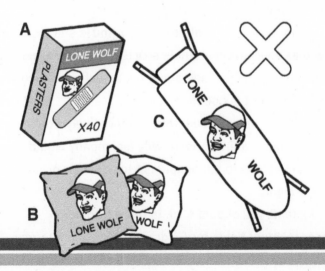

ENDORSEMENTS

When you reach the big league of motorsport you can expect your profile to soar and that means the opening of another potentially lucrative avenue: endorsements.

Your manager will guide you carefully towards the products or services that will provide a 'best fit', as long as you understand that the 'best' thing they want to 'fit' is 'more money' into their 'bank account'.

In the 1970s it was perfectly acceptable for a driver to endorse cigarettes and alcoholic beverages because they were consuming lots of them anyway and doing so in public meant they'd get sent more of them in the post. Today, however, you must be more careful of where you allow your face to be plastered.

Aligning yourself with a booze brand is still okay, as long as your involvement is strictly limited to a weirdly self-defeating message about not actually drinking any of the product in question.

If you're uneasy about this or, more likely, you're completely confused about why a company would spend millions to tell people not to use their products, steer clear.

Instead, you should stick to more traditional endorsement fields for F1 drivers such as motor car accessories, sports bags or random food stuffs in the country you are from.

The latter can be a source of great joy for fans from overseas as, for example, they find themselves on holiday in your home country and discover with great delight that you are the face of the nation's second favourite brand of chocolate spread. They may even take a picture of this and post it on social media, which is basically free advertising for the product and for you, as long as they don't caption the picture with something about you being a 'sell-out' who is 'hawking crap'.

On this note, do remember to pay as much attention as you can muster to the endorsement deals that you are signing rather than simply autographing a contract and then noticing that your manager has a new Aston Martin.

Without occasionally checking what exactly you're endorsing you might one day find your PA is telling you that today you're needed in Antwerp for six hours where, you discover with a sinking feeling, you're making a corporate film at the low-key HQ of a company that mines blood diamonds. This is not a good look, especially if it later turns out that the company also belongs to your dad.

YOUR PERSONAL BRAND

Merchandising and endorsements are wonderful things for an F1 driver but they can be so much more effective if you have a strong personal brand.

That means working out what's distinctive and interesting about you.

Unfortunately, as a modern sports person there might not be anything distinctive and interesting about you at all.

On the off chance there is, try to work out what it is you want to push about yourself.

Here, for example, are some brands you might want to consider, if appropriate:

- **The fast one**
- **The cool one**
- **The funny one**
- **The intense one**
- **The one who appears not to give a toss**

Obviously, a lot of your personal brand comes from how people perceive you and that can be a hard thing to manipulate because fans can detect immediately that you are not a wild and crazy guy just because you've grown a beard and almost said a swearword in an interview. There is every chance that your personal brand will emerge as something beyond your control, which might be fine.

On the other hand, it might be something you want to quash before it gets out of hand.

If you wish to be an F1 champion, the following are some personal brands you probably want to get some consultant in to smother, pronto:

- **The one who crashes a lot**

- **The one who said that thing on the radio that one time and now it's all anyone remembers about them**

- **The one who is only there because he brings a load of cash from an enormous corporation in his home country**

- **The one who isn't as good as that other one**

- **The one who is just making up the numbers and will never win a world title**

- **The one with that rumour about a dog**

SOCIAL MEDIA

Social media is a powerful way for a Formula One driver to communicate directly with fans.

Typically, these are the sort of messages your fans will expect (because it's what all other drivers do, for some reason):

- Telling people you're in the gym (which is every day, but anyway ...)

- Telling people you're in a nicer place than them (e.g. beach, private jet, exclusive party)

- Telling people you've had a great day with the guys from [name of company that pays you to endorse their product] learning all about the great new [slightly different version of the product]

- Telling people you've been for an extremely long bike ride (extra points if it was with another driver or ex-driver or a person who cycles for a living)

- Telling people you've had a 'great day at the office' while posting a picture of something that is patently not an office, such as another beach or the cockpit of your racing car

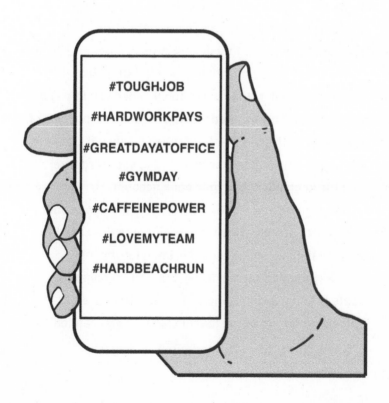

WHERE TO LIVE

Now you're in F1 you need to live like an F1 driver (i.e. not with your parents).

Basically, you have two options. If you want to be a real pro and a complete team player you will live near the factory which, with a few exceptions, means living in the English Midlands. This is fine, although if you're from, say, Seville you will eventually find yourself trudging miserably around Towcester in the rain wondering where to find decent presa ibérica.

The other problem with living in the UK is that the government will rather unreasonably ask you to pay tax on your suddenly inflated income. If you find this part of the social contract distasteful then you should consider moving to somewhere more suited to your largesse and the keeping of it in your bank account.

If in general you like living in Britain then you could try the Isle of Man, which offers all of the drizzle with none of the tax liabilities and is ideal for the more dismally minded racing driver, but a more common route is to try Switzerland or Monaco. Both are extremely boring but at least in Monaco you can look at the sea.

DO say, 'I'm sorry I was late to the grid ceremony as we were taking care of some last-minute strategy.'

DON'T say, 'I was taking a shit.'

DO say, 'For sure, this is a learning experience and I think we're going to build on what we take away from here today.'

DON'T say, 'The car is crap and I don't want to do this any more.'

ROAD CARS

When it comes to road cars, Formula One drivers tend to fall into one of two categories.

1. **Really interested in road cars because they're cool and sexy and it's something to blow spare cash on.**

2. **Not interested in road cars at all because you've fired towards Parabolica at 200mph and felt the plank scuff the ground on the way into Eau Rouge and frankly anything else is boring after that.**

If you are type 1 then soon after entering F1 you must go out and buy an exceptionally rare and powerful hypercar in which you can immediately have an extremely embarrassing low-speed accident, preferably involving an old lady in a small Citroën which injures no one but still costs you £100,000 in damage repairs.

Once you have got this out of your system, you can then settle down to amassing a nice collection of supercars and sought-after classics, none of which you can talk about as they're not made by anyone affiliated with your current team.

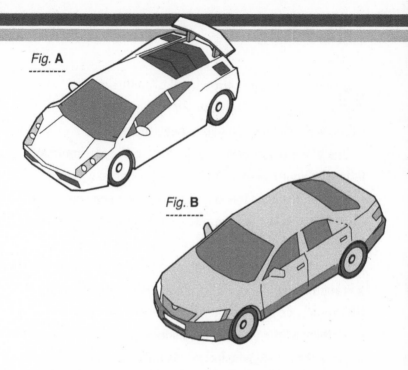

Fig. **A**

Fig. **B**

If you are type 2 then you will be happy to accept a free example of whatever moderately dreary saloon car or SUV the road car company affiliated to your team wants you to have. All you have to do is drive it when you need to get somewhere and try to remember its name if you're ever asked about it in the press (bonus points if you can manage to do so while sounding enthusiastic).

Hey presto, before you know it they'll have named a limited edition of their tepid hatchback model after you, not that you'll really care or indeed have noticed.

CLOTHES

Once you reach the top level of motor racing you're going to have more money and, as is the ironic way of things, more access to free stuff.

One of the results of this is that you can experiment a little with your clothes, and this can be a good way to raise your profile in those rare moments when you're not head-to-toe in Nomex overalls or branded teamwear.

Most racing drivers do not seize this opportunity and continue to spend their downtime dressed like a kid from a Frankfurt high school who's really into computers. Or they mostly do this, but then occasionally decide to try something a little unusual for a special event and end up looking like a child who forced his parents to buy the most expensive fancy-dress outfit in the shop.

But you don't have to be like this (although you probably will because F1 drivers typically have terrible dress sense, as if the G-forces involved in high-speed driving damage the part of your brain that rejects chinos). You want to be F1 champion, right? So why not dress like a champion.

Go nuts. Experiment a little. Become fashion forward. Turn up to an awards ceremony in a tartan matador jacket and a sarong? Why not! This is the sort of thing that makes you a star and propels you on to being a winner.

If you take a few risks with your clothes the world outside motor racing will start to notice you.

And it will say, oh yeah, him, isn't he the guy who dresses like he ran into a charity shop and put on the first five things he could find?

WATCHES

Watches are a big part of Formula One.

Partly this is because it's all about times and is therefore considered a 'good fit' in watch-company marketing departments, and partly it's because people who enjoy watching cars drive round in circles also seem to enjoy extremely expensive wrist jewellery that performs a function you get for free on your phone.

As soon as you arrive in F1 you're going to want to get a slice of that sweet, sweet freebie wrist-clock action, but a word to the wise: whether you're walking into a team that already has a tasty watch sponsor on board or you're urging your manager to go out and get you a personal deal, the likelihood is that you'll be strapping on a really, really chunky watch at all times when you're not driving.

No, seriously, it's going to be massive. That way it shows up on TV coverage better.

Also, if you've gone for a personal sponsorship arrangement, it's probably with one of those companies that makes the ultra-expensive and highly noticeable watches favoured by leathery sex pests who hang around harbours in places like Monaco and Puerto Banús, and wearing it will feel like you've had Elton John's kitchen clock taped to your arm.

As such, remember to adjust your gym routine accordingly, otherwise you'll end up with uneven arms.

FACIAL HAIR

F1 has a proud history of facial hair and the cultivation of a less-shaved part of your face is definitely something you should consider in your quest to be a champion.

Here are some avenues you could pursue.

MASSIVE SIDEYS

Proven triple
championship power
from the 1970s.

PENCIL MOUSTACHE

Elegantly reach for
glory with some
1950s face fuzz.
Ding dong!

• *SOUP STRAINER*

World championship winning power. Warning: will not suppress endless moaning.

• *CHIN STRAP*

Multi-championship winning potential. Might also make you look a bit of a tit.

UNRULY BUMFLUFF

Not an especially strong look, though it does suggest you spend so long on strategy and set-up that you've no time to pop down to Boots for new razors.

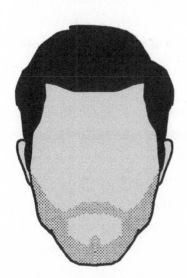

STUBBLE

Not practical. It just gets stuck to your Nomex balaclava like crazy Velcro.

LOVE INTEREST

It's amazing how being in F1 makes you suddenly more attractive.

It's certainly rare to meet a Formula One racer who isn't draped in models whenever they feel like it. Now you're in F1, you might want to do the same but after a while you might just want a full-time girlfriend.

Let's assume for now you're a straight white man. After all, there are no female drivers in F1 because, come on, it's only 2019 – and weirdly there are no gay men.

(Okay, statistically there must be and it's almost as if one or two drivers are pretending to be straight because the sport is built on a bedrock of old, and old-fashioned, men who don't like 'that sort of thing' and your career would suffer horribly if you came out.)

Anyway, being an F1 driver and having a girlfriend is a tremendous idea for a number of reasons.

It means you have someone more glamourous to take to public events, deflecting attention from the fact that you're the kind of guy who goes to the public opening of a new club in Cannes wearing a branded polo shirt.

It means the TV cameras have someone nice-looking to focus on, standing in the back of the pit garage looking chic during boring bits of a race. And of course it means you've got someone to take Instagram photos of you.

Plus, having a lady on your arm will definitely help to bat away any rumours that you're actually not interested in ladies (see above).

Conversely, having a girlfriend might be a distraction from your quest to be F1 champion.

She might want to talk to you about dinner plans when you're desperately trying to think about your qualifying set-up. She almost certainly won't be that interested when you're proudly explaining how you shaved another 0.07 seconds off your best time at Silverstone. And she might be an aspiring singer and might want to play you some of her new songs, and they might be terrible.

Best advice: maybe stay focused on your aspirations for the season and, if you're feeling lonely, ask your manager to send over another busload of swimwear models.

HOW TO TALK TO THE MEDIA

Since the invention of social media, the regular media is no longer an F1 driver's only means of communication with fans and the public at large (although the press will report on things you put on social media too so do bear this in mind before you say something a bit daft online and then have to delete your entire Instagram for a bit).

Despite the change in the media landscape, the press is still very important to F1, which is why each race venue has a special room full of slightly overweight middle-aged men acting with studied indifference and not reporting the real gossip they've heard because they don't want to have their season-long press pass taken away.

Since the old-fashioned press is still so important in F1, it's equally important that you learn how to talk to journalists. This is what you need to remember.

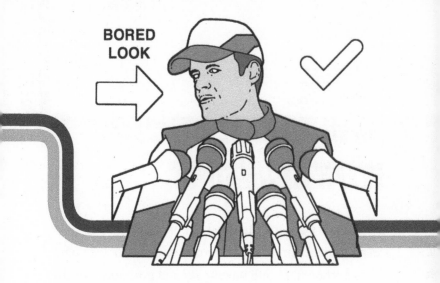

BORED LOOK

For print media interviews:

1. Adopt an air of utter resignation and boredom.

2. Don't say anything interesting.

However, for TV interviews the rules are very different, as follows:

1. Start every other sentence with 'for sure'.

2. Don't say anything interesting.

That's pretty much it.

HOW TO DEAL WITH SPONSORS

Sponsors are the lifeblood of Formula One and without them the sport would spend a lot less on fancy carbon fibre and hospitality and probably have to hold more races on Saturdays at Thruxton.

Basically, F1 would become BTCC. If you don't want that to happen then you must be nice to the sponsors.

That means not shouting 'Get all these stupid people out of my garage' as yet another gaggle of dithering American businessmen stumble through your pit in the lead-up to free practice two.

That means not complaining when you have to spend an entire afternoon in an airless film studio near Daventry wearing branded clothing and pretending to enjoy drinking a beverage that tastes like cough medicine sieved through a wet sock.

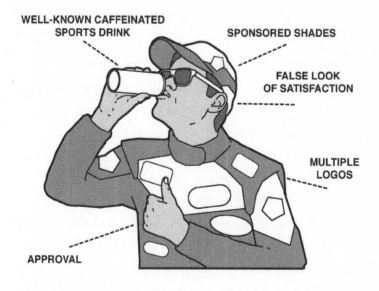

WELL-KNOWN CAFFEINATED SPORTS DRINK

SPONSORED SHADES

FALSE LOOK OF SATISFACTION

MULTIPLE LOGOS

APPROVAL

That means smiling cheerfully and posing for a lot of selfies when you're contractually obliged to spend an evening in Dusseldorf at the grand opening of a new regional logistics and processing centre.

These are the things sponsors will expect from you. And these are the things you will have to give them. Because they are the sponsors. And they have the money.

FANS

Fans are a vital part of the world of an aspiring F1 champion.

'This one was for the fans,' you might say after a hard-won victory. 'I couldn't have done this without the fans,' you'll gush breathlessly as you collect your first championship trophy.

This is, of course, bollocks. Technically, you could have done all of it without fans.

Fans did not buy your first kart, nor design your Formula One car, nor pay for its construction and shipping around the world. Yes, yes, if they bought a team cap or shirt they did a little bit, but they're not exactly China's fourth-largest meat-processing conglomerate and they aren't laying down millions a year to make all this happen.

It's probably best not to mention this when you meet the fans, which inevitably you will have to. They'll be there, crowded behind barriers at the entrance to the paddock, outside your hotel when you just want to get inside for an early night, shivering in the car park when you're booked for a personal appearance at a drizzly Silverstone on a cold Tuesday in January.

And just look at the state of them. You wear head-to-toe team kit because you have to. These people paid for theirs. Why would they do that?

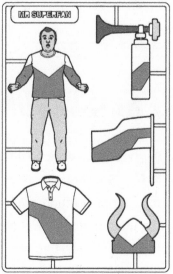

Well, because there's something they see in you that perhaps doesn't draw them to any of the other people on the grid. A twinkle in your eye, a spring in your step, a promise in your talent. Maybe it's your looks, maybe it's the insane overtaking move you pulled off against that guy everyone thought was a dick in Formula Two. These fans chose you, and sometimes you have to pay it back. Shake the hands, pose for the selfies, sign the programmes.

And then, as you come round that last corner on that last lap and half the grandstand erupts into a cheer so loud you can hear it over your engine you will realise that, oh wow yes, the fans are important. So try to be nice to them, won't you?

PRE-SEASON TESTING

Here we are then. You're an F1 driver.

The contracts have been signed, you've been for your seat fitting, you've done the photoshoot with the team mate you will soon learn to hate. Now down to business, starting with the all-important pre-season testing.

You've driven the new car already, of course, but only in the simulator back at the factory, and the simulator doesn't suddenly lose power through a fast corner on the far side of the track or attempt to electrocute you when you get out. That's what makes pre-season so exciting: you get to try the real car for the first time and there's an outside chance it might try to kill you.

Pre-season testing is a hugely important way to get to know the new car while it still isn't working properly, so you can get a feel for what you'll be driving for the rest of the year and the engineers can get an idea of why it's still making that weird buzzing sound.

For teams, pre-season testing is a vital part of the de-bugging and set-up process. For outsiders and the media, it's a chance to see the cars in action and then make speculation about what this means for the season, even though everyone knows you can't gather much from a test session and, as such, they're completely wasting their breath.

Naturally, journalists will want to ask you how testing went and the general form is to reply in one of two ways:

1. **We're not taking anything for granted. You know, some of our rivals are looking really strong. (Real meaning: The car is insanely fast but we're sandbagging like crazy and playing it cool.)**

2. **Yeah, for sure, there is a long way to go but we're really happy with what we've got so far. (Real meaning: The car feels terrible and I'm already depressed.)**

HOW TO CELEBRATE ON THE PODIUM

If all goes well, sometime during your first season you're going to find yourself on the podium.

Of course, you'll have been there before in the lower formulas but the Formula One podium is different. There are lots of people watching this time, and they play more music for some reason.

Obviously, if you find yourself on the podium the giddy rush of adrenaline may make it difficult to think straight but please bear in mind the following:

- Savour the moment

- Try not to get splashback on the local dignitary who just gave you your trophy

- Remember to spray champagne in the face of one of the other drivers in a way that might be playful or might be the physical manifestation of your feelings about him (i.e. you think he's a dick)

- Don't hold the bottle in a way that looks like you're urinating on the crowd below

- Glug back some of the bottle contents, but not so much that you get a bit giddy and fall over the railings

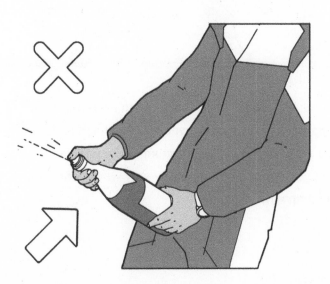

Also, if you have a chance, try to think of a special
gimmick that will make you stand out and endear you
to the crowd, e.g. a memorable dance or arm
movement or a revoltingly sweaty way of consuming
champagne.

EXCUSES

You were in racing long enough before you got to F1 to know that the most important thing a racing driver needs is excuses.

Whenever your qualifying position is dismal, whenever your race is a total washout because you ran wide on lap 2, whenever you crash out after an incident with your team mate, you need to have an excuse.

Here are some classics, in case you need them.

- **The set-up hasn't been great all weekend**

- **We're just not getting heat into these tyres**

- **We're definitely down on power compared to the others**

- **Maybe the organisers need to look at the design of the new chicane**

- **I don't want to point the finger but I hope someone else is asking a few questions of themselves right now**

Above all, remember one thing: it is never, ever, ever your fault.

Even though, obviously, sometimes it is.

THE SEASON

So this is it. It's here. You're in F1. You have your eyes on the prize.

The only problem is, so do 19 other people. And some of them aren't deluding themselves.

Your first F1 season is, as commentators always say in that way they use in montages to get people excited about the new season, LIGHTS OUT AND GO, GO, GO.

Now, an F1 season is long and with many, many twists and turns but do please try to incorporate at least some of the following into yours:

- Incident with backmarker that will ruin very promising performance in one race
- Mechanical failure at worst possible time
- Pit-stop disaster
- Extraordinary good fortune
- Extraordinary misfortune
- Incident with team mate that will overshadow run-up to summer break
- Series of bad starts that will make people question your skill
- Breath-taking overtaking move that will make people forget about the above
- Tedious procession in which you will plod round in exactly the same place for the entire race and barely appear on TV coverage
- Something that makes commentators witter on about the 'undercut'

That's the sort of business you should make your business. You will duck, you will dodge, you will give interviews in which you say 'It's not over yet' or 'For sure, it's been tough', or you just give one of those very long sighs that makes you sound like a deflating spaniel.

THE SEASON ENDS

After all of the travel and the training and the dedication to a cause that has been your life's work, the season will draw to a close and one of two things will have happened ...

1. YEEEEEEEES! You are F1 champion.

2. Oh dear. You are not F1 champion.

If option 1 then let the good times roll.

Spray champagne, do a little dance, release several Instagram pictures of you standing against a sunset on the deck of a yacht. You are the Formula One world champion.

1

2

On that note, if you're going to win the title could you try to do it in a nail-biting, down-to-the-last-race contest with another driver in which you seal the deal with a hard-fought victory? Something like that.

More to the point, do your best not to claim your title in one of those tedious maths-based ways where you clinch it by grabbing fourth place in the third-from-last race of the season and you're not even on the podium to celebrate.

Obviously, this is largely pointless advice because you're a racing driver and you just want to win at any cost but if you have a moment try to remember what it's like to watch this stuff on the telly at home.

Anyway, however you've won, enjoy it. Savour it. There will never be another moment in your life quite like that first championship so drink it in like so much slightly warm, fizzy wine from the oversized bottle of delight. This is your moment and you must bask in it for all its worth.

Obviously, it will be hard to articulate how this feels, but that won't stop endless TV interviewers from asking.

Here's a tip: instead of trying to put into words a giddy, dizzying adrenaline rush made from the pure essence of your entire life's ambition, why not simply shout, 'WHOOO!' and then pivot away from the camera into an elaborate breakdance? It'll take some pulling off but it's got to be more interesting than saying 'It's an amazing feeling' for the 12th time.

Again, think about how this will look on TV. It will look incredible. Especially if you do a drop into the splits and then spring back up into a 360-degree spin. Yeah!

Oh dear, no wait, it's option 2, isn't it?

Now either a world title was never on the cards because your car was lousy and your luck was non-existent, in which case spend the off-season nagging your manager to find you another team despite your watertight two-year deal, or you were in the fight and it just didn't go your way.

If that was the scenario, your tone in interviews must be despondent, dejected and distracted, but with just a hint of optimism for next year (which is entirely fake because really you're furious and next year might as well be two centuries away). It's a tricky tone to hit, so why not practise this in front of a mirror?

The main thing is that, first of all, you need to get some excuses out there – the other guys just seemed stronger, we never recovered from those early-season issues, we definitely need to look at our strategy calls, etc., etc. – remembering at all times to say 'we' while making it pretty clear you believe all of this was the fault of other people. As the old expression goes, 'There's no "I" in "blame the team".'

After that, retire to lick your wounds, remembering that nothing makes metaphorical wounds heal faster than being on board a yacht with lots of people in bikinis. A brief bit of post-season time off and then you're all ready to bound back into the factory to demand that they make you a faster car for next year.

Because there's always next year.

DO wear a branded team cap at all times.

DON'T slouch about the paddock in a hat that says HARD ROCK CAFÉ ANTWERP on the front just because you 'like it'.

DO leap from your car at the end of a race like an especially agile cat.

DON'T get tangled up in all the drinks tubes and comms wires and end up stumbling out of the cockpit like a drunk being attacked by wasps.

MOVING TO ANOTHER TEAM

At some point in a Formula One driver's life they are probably going to move to a different team.

This could be good news for you, just as it'll be bad news for those fans who've bought a wardrobe full of branded merchandise in the colours of the old team (although this will be less of an issue if they're one of those fans that has confused F1 with football and supports the team above all).

There are various reasons for leaving your existing team and these are the main ones.

1. **You have decided to go because you've found a different team that's better.**

2. **The team has decided to get rid of you because they've found a different driver who's better.**

3. **There's been a falling out because you ratted on the team or called them all idiots.**

Obviously you should have publicly shown great loyalty to your old team and said you were 'totally committed' to them ... right up until the moment you signed the contract with the new place. At which point you have to make a bit of a fuss about how excited you are even if, thanks to reasons 2 or 3 above, you've had to join them despite the fact that they're generally considered to be worse.

If your new team has been around for ages and wins things, or used to, remember to say that you are humbled by the history.

If they're new, or it's an old team that's been completely re-branded for lots of complicated reasons that mean they want to forget all about what went before, just remember to say that everything is 'exciting' and a 'fresh opportunity', at least until the first test session when the car turns up late and then completes just four laps because it doesn't work properly.

ANOTHER TRY

Whether you've got that first F1 championship or not, soon after the season ends and you've got bored of sitting on the Med having your protein shakes made by a winsome social media star in a sarong, you're going to need to get back in the saddle.

Not literally. Horses are dangerous and nothing curtails off-season training like a broken neck.

Start your winter regime by filling social media with lots of photos of you in the gym, thereby implying, in a sort of static version of the montage in a boxing movie, that you are coming back fitter and stronger and more determined than ever.

Seal the deal by giving a press interview in which you talk a good game about being 'more focused' and 'more determined' than ever. However, try to stop short of saying you really think this could be your year because this is the kind of thing that will come back and bite you on the bottom when it later turns out that this was not, in fact, your year on account of it belonging to someone else who won more races than you.

The main point is that it's always good to get into a positive frame of mind before the next season, even if you're the reigning world champion.

Unless, of course, you decide that fighting for another title just sounds like far too much stress and aggro and you announce your retirement from the sport. It's not a very racing driver thing to do, unless you're one of those racing drivers who never much seemed to enjoy being a racing driver in the first place.

THE
AFTERMATH

LIFE AFTER F1

No one can be a Formula One driver forever, though some have tried.

It doesn't matter how many championships you've won or lost, one day you're just going to have to realise that your time is done.

Actually, you don't have to realise this at all: the teams will do it for you via the simple expedient of no longer offering you employment.

Obviously you can pre-empt this by announcing your retirement, although it will be pretty obvious to fans and the media if you're 'retiring' because you're genuinely too old and tired to put up with this nonsense any more or if you're making this announcement because you know there's nowhere for you to go, like someone loudly declaring that they're not going to attend a party they weren't invited to in the first place.

The point is, whether your departure from the sport happens with dignity or not, don't worry, because there are plenty of things for an ex-F1 driver – especially a former world champion – to do with themselves in the career afterlife.

Here are some options.

● *ENDURANCE RACING*

After the intense rigours of F1 you need a break from all that speed and G-force, so why not make a move into the relaxing world of eight hours in the car at full racing speed and half of that time at night?

Endurance racing, most famously demonstrated by the 24 Hours of Le Mans, is a great home for a retired F1 driver because, like F1, it requires immense skill and stamina but, unlike F1, seems quite content to let people in their 40s and 50s compete.

Take that, ageism.

● INDY 500

As a nation America isn't that interested in Formula One, and that's because it has lots of motorsport of its own.

The most prestigious of US events is the Indianapolis 500, which requires a new set of skills. However, they can't be that hard to pick up because some people who seemed like right no-hopers in F1 have won it. This is part of a noble tradition of outsiders (i.e. not Americans) popping over to the US and winning the Indy 500.

This presumably irritates American race fans quite a lot so don't expect to become a household name, at least not without your actual name becoming prefaced by the word 'goddam'.

• *FORMULA E*

Formula E is the new, up-and-coming electric race series that fans are duty-bound to remind people is 'getting better'.

It's also a useful refuge for former F1 drivers, especially those who are keen to try something new or found the old cars too noisy anyway.

For ex-Formula One stars it's clearly a bit slow and tame but Formula E has got some cash and you get to travel, so just remember not to twitch slightly as you cheerily endorse something you're clearly not that into.

● *TOURING CARS*

If you were known for always crashing into other
drivers you might be delighted to learn there's a special
racing series that'll suit your style.

It's rare for an ex-F1 person to enter this formula
because all the cars look like saloons and it feels like
going into minicabbing but try it, you might like it –
especially if you enjoy using another car as a brake
and spending a disproportionate amount of your time
at Thruxton.

● *TELEVISION*

If your driving days are well and truly over, why not make the move into TV, where you may not be able to do any driving but you can at least talk about it with some authority?

If you can do so in an articulate and interesting way, and in a pleasant tone that doesn't sound like someone monotonously reading out a list of lost luggage, all the better.

The classic path for an ex-F1 star in TV is to become a pundit on the Formula One coverage. This gives you the chance to stand around in a neatly pressed shirt that's firmly tucked into some smart-casual trousers holding a stick microphone like it's a lollipop while a disembodied voice in your ear says, 'Coming to you next.'

TV is a great opportunity for a former driver as it keeps you in the public eye (which is good for still getting free stuff like nice watches), it allows you to share your experience and you might get promoted to co-commentator, which will allow you to use that experience to calmly humiliate the actual commentator when they get a bit carried away with their speculation because they're just a glorified radio DJ and you once banged it past someone on the outside of Curva Grande.

● DRIVER MANAGEMENT

If you can't drive any more, why not show the world your keen eye for talent and determination by finding a prodigy and becoming their manager?

You can use all your experience and knowledge to help them in their career and one day perhaps they too could be a Formula One driver and even an F1 champion.

All you have to do is teach them not to make the mistakes you made, apart from the one about giving their manager 20 per cent of their income, plus a separate negotiation for merch revenues.

● *YOUR OWN TEAM*

You know F1. You were in F1. You were an F1 champion, for flip's sake. You could run an F1 team. Of course you could.

What could be difficult about that, apart from having to manage vast numbers of people while worrying about the financial and logistical elements of the operation and plotting business strategies beyond the confines of 20-odd races a year?

In actual fact, running a Formula One team is really hard, and this is demonstrated by all the people who have made an absolute arse of it over the years.

As an ex-driver there is no reason to think you will do any better or worse, except that, at heart, you're a racing driver and therefore have literally no attention span and possibly very little interest in others.

If you really must go ahead with something like this just remember that, as an ex-driver, you will either have to buy an existing team (which will then go bust) or set up something from scratch (which won't go brilliantly until it is bought by someone else and becomes the best team on the grid, but only a long, long time after you were involved).

THE COMEBACK

What if retirement doesn't mean retirement? What if an opportunity opens up and you have a chance to return to F1?

Yes, these younger pups have got all the big ideas and the bravery but that's the folly of youth. They don't have your experience and your wisdom and that's got to count for a lot. You were quick in your day, you can be quick again, especially if you combine your raw skill with your age-won smarts.

Is this it? Is this the time for a glorious comeback and, who knows, even another shot at the world title?

No. It is not. This kind of thing never ends well.

ENDORSEMENTS AND INVESTMENTS

The good news is that, whether you do any or all of the above (or not), you're a former F1 driver and that has a surprising amount of currency out in the commercial world.

Plus, now your spare hours aren't taken up doing adverts and personal appearances for your team's big sponsors you'll have much more time to pursue more of those lucrative personal deals. Spokesperson for a megayacht company, non-executive chairman of a bauxite mining concern, the public face of a new kind of Belgian whisky – there's no limit to the things you can put your name to in return for large amounts of money.

Another bonus: you can use some of that money to invest in things that interest you, such as making more money and saying yes to people who promise they can do that for you.

Now is the time to pursue that investment portfolio you've always dreamt of, which is diffuse and bizarre and includes property, aftershave, a marquee hire company in Nice and two kinds of olive oil.

MOTIVATIONAL SPEAKING

Allowing makers of wine, jet-skis and cat repellent to put your face on their promotional literature in return for cash is all well and good, but don't ignore other avenues that might open up as a result of the glamourous miasma that surrounds you because you used to be in Formula One.

One such avenue is the potentially lucrative world of motivational speaking. Big corporations love this kind of stuff and, as you should well know, big corporations have big pockets full of big amounts of money.

So next time Securitrexe Insurance want to get their northern European sales conference amped up to smash last year's targets, what could be better than bringing on someone who knows all about winning? Yes, that's you. And all you have to do is put together a stirring speech with lots of references to 'teamwork', 'goals' and 'strategies for excellence'.

That's essential, by the way. You can't expect to keep trousering fat sacks of cash if you just run onto the stage clapping your hands together like a seal and shouting, 'WOO! YEAH! SELL! OKAY!' and then run off again.

RANDOM BUSINESSES

You've been in F1. You're a champion (hopefully). There's nothing you can't do.

Or so you think.

So if you've ever wanted to own a car dealership or an airline or a yoghurt factory, now's your chance. What can possibly go wrong?

Well, that's for you to find out.

Clue: quite a lot, actually.

CONCLUSION

Becoming an F1 driver is hard.

Becoming F1 champion is even harder.

It's as tricky as joining the SAS or leaving the royal family, or trying to leave the royal family to become a member of the SAS.

Look at it this way: since 1950 a total of 857 people have taken part in F1 races, and most of them were really good. However, just 33 of those people have become F1 champion, and only one of those wasn't extremely good. Alright, maybe two.

But don't give up hope. After all, every year *someone* has to be F1 champion, so why couldn't it be you? Perhaps because you were given this book for Christmas and you're a 57-year-old butcher. But perhaps not.

Perhaps you're already a racing driver. Perhaps it could be you.

Oh wait, you're a racing driver. You have the attention span of an exhausted toddler and you flicked straight to the back of this book hoping to find that the answer was contained on the very last page. Well, it's not. Go back and read the whole thing.

And remember, you can do this!

You can read a book!

Or you can get your manager to read out the whole thing while you're on the cross trainer.

GOOD LUCK!